SENSE POETRY

WISH UPON A STAR

First published in Great Britain in 2025 by:

Young Writers
Remus House
Coltsfoot Drive
Peterborough
PE2 9BF
Telephone: 01733 890066
Website: www.youngwriters.co.uk

All Rights Reserved
Book Design by Ashley Janson
© Copyright Contributors 2025
Softback ISBN 978-1-83685-789-1
Printed and bound in the UK by BookPrintingUK
Website: www.bookprintinguk.com
YB0652K

FOREWORD

Welcome to this book packed full of sights and smells, sounds and tastes!

Young Writers' Sense Poetry competition was specifically designed as a fun introduction to poetry and as a way for children to think about the senses: what these poets can see, taste, smell, touch and hear in the world around them. From this starting point, the poems could be as simple or as elaborate as the writer wanted, using imagination and descriptive language to conjure a multifaceted image of the subject of their writing, rather than concentrating just on what it looks like.

Here at Young Writers, we believe that seeing their work in print will inspire a love of reading and writing and give these young poets the confidence to develop their skills in the future. Poetry is a wonderful way to introduce young children to the idea of rhyme and rhythm and helps learning and development of communication, language and literacy skills.

With poems on a whole range of subjects from animals and everyday objects to emotions and the world around them, these young poets have used their creative writing abilities, sentence structure skills, thoughtful vocabulary and most importantly, their imaginations, to make their poems come alive. I hope you enjoy reading them as much as we have.

CONTENTS

Independent Entrants

Tahnée Heagarty-Grant (7)   1

Kingsley Primary School, Northampton

Megan Pham (6)   3
Eden Krupnik (6)   4
Andreea Mirea (7)   5

Marlborough Infant School, Small Heath

Zayaan Ahmed (7)   6
Taibah Sarfraz (7)   7
Muhammad Raiyan Zaman (6)   8
Ibraheem Ramzan (6)   9
Mohamed-Amin Salad (7)   10
Ruqaya Mohamed (7)   11
Binyamin Toseef (7)   12
Salihah Mahmood (6)   13
Hanifah Husayn (6)   14
Saleha Zaman (6)   15
Rayyan Ismail Ayub (7)   16
Ayaan Nawab Khan (6)   17
Inaaya Khan (7)   18
Fatima Ayoka Hassan (7)   19
Laiba Fatima (7)   20
Haytham Zariet (7)   21
Mahir N (6)   22
Yasin Rahman (6)   23
Adiba Syeda Tasnim (7)   24
Areesha Shirin (7)   25
Asadallah Muset (7)   26
Khadija Islam (7)   27

Moeez Bashir (7)   28
Rehan Ali Shah (6) & Inaaya Zeb (6)   29
Jabbar Hussain (6)   30
Abdullah Haqqanee (6)   31
Nishan Singh (7)   32
Mohammed Shiras Khan (7)   33
Safa Kosar (7), Sofia (7), Denisa (7) & Umair Muhammed (7)   34
Umar Muhammad (7)   35
Abrish Saqib (6)   36
Yousaf Khan (7)   37
Muzamil Wafa (6)   38
Zainab Zahra (7)   39
Mustafa Khan (6)   40

Penryn Primary Academy, Penryn

Lilymae Jaggers (6)   41
David Seredin (7)   42
Laudus Nesbitt (7)   43
Ezekiel Demery (7)   44
Eva Festorazzi (7)   45
Mya Nicholas (7)   46
Zac Dawe (7)   47
Archie Sargant (6)   48
Helena Blay (7)   49
Elliot Adams (7)   50
Arthur Williams (6)   51
Meilah Gauld (7)   52
Fflur Hoban (7)   53
Loulou Huebner (7)   54
Leo Nankivell (7)   55
Adelyn Knowles (6)   56
Scarlett Buringham (7)   57
Esmae Vincent (7)   58

Ethan Harwood (7)	59
Mia-Elaine Collick (6)	60
Seren Jordon (7)	61
Owen Brown (7)	62
Alfee Reid (7)	63
Dougie Boughton Rowe (7)	64
Rory Darroch-Lassey (7)	65
Lloyd Jackman (7)	66
Albie Price (6)	67
Henry Parkinson (7)	68
Frankie Blundell (7)	69
Evie Pattison (7)	70
Grayson Rohleder (6)	71
Penny Brenton (6)	72

Radford Semele CofE Primary School, Leamington Spa

Alfred Hudson (6)	73

Shipbourne School, Shipbourne

Gabriela Traczynska (7)	74
Finley Groves (6)	75
Bluebell Martin (6)	76
Patrick Crowhurst (7)	77
Esme Martin (6)	78
Christopher Hayton-Vernet (6)	79
Rosie Baker (7)	80
Isabella Wallace (7)	81

Stratford-Sub-Castle CE Primary School, Stratford-Sub-Castle

Jasmine Varney (7)	82
Lori Legg (6)	83
Zoey Lumby (7)	84
Charlie Ormshaw (6)	85
Phoebe Lake (7)	86
Samuel Murphy (7)	87
Sophia Badcock (6)	88
Arthur Elkins (6)	89
Matilda Crespo (7)	90
Cody Hull (7)	91

Lydia Kennedy (6)	92
Ronan Paton (7)	93
Fern Rusbridge (7)	94
Esther Ewing (7)	95
Francesca Gibson (5)	96
Martha Maclean (7)	97
Nancy Cash (6)	98
Leo Sawyer (7)	99
Sophie Hislop (5)	100
Grace Cash (6)	101
Zara Altin (7)	102
Christiano Ayodeji (6)	103
Aneurin Faulkner (6)	104
Rory Ferguson (6)	105
Hollie Blake (7)	106
Rae Goody (5)	107
Reggie Chant (6)	108
Cruz Lampe (6)	109
Louis Doe (6)	110
Arthur Goldring (6)	111
Logan Borsos-Grenier (7)	112

The Lantern Community Primary School, Ely

Chloe Harper (6)	113
Emily Curry (6)	114
Elora Vadamootoo (6)	115
Imogen Harris (6)	116
Zola Brown (6)	117
Aria McCabe (6)	118
Caleb Martin (6)	119
Sophie Howlett (6)	120
Evelyn Young (5)	121
Max Law (5)	122
Hector Williams (5)	123
Lorelei Couzins (6)	124
Linus MacKenzie-Oakes (6)	125
George Langford (6)	126
Frank McCreadie (6)	127
Erin Vivash-Ball (6)	128
Olive Hatton (5)	129
Violet Milne (6)	130
Millie Stammers (5)	131

Cooper Platt (6)	132
Reese Rose (6)	133
Axel Bliss (6)	134
Ellinor Johnson (6)	135
Charlotte Lloyd (6)	136
Odette Munganyika (6)	137
Rupert Halls (6)	138
Beth Harvey (6)	139
Harry Skinner (6)	140
Ollie Beale (6)	141
Benjamin Rowlands (6)	142
Rafe Maudsley-Noble (6)	143
Freddie Godsmark (5)	144
Erin Holmes (6)	145
Jake Downton (6)	146
Alex Curtis (5)	147
Alex Southward (6)	148
Logan Jenkins (5)	149
Robert Hughes (6)	150
Paul Musson (5)	151
Eleanor Mullins (6)	152
Leo Cattani-Price (6)	153
Elijah Mekwuye (6)	154
Adam Nash (6)	155
Avighna Verma (6)	156
Evelyn House (6)	157
Aurora Turner (5)	158
Oliver Gunbie (6)	159
Seraphina Atkins (5)	160
Daniel Ching (6)	161
Jensen Green (5)	162

THE POEMS

The Beautiful Beach

I *see* blue, thrashing, giant waves crashing against bumpy, black rocks.
I *hear* people laughing, watching videos of seagulls stealing food.
I *smell* a yummy barbecue, 'mmm smells so good, I want to eat it now'.
I *feel* the cold, swishing wind going through my golden locks and hot, burning sand between my little toes.
I *taste* creamy, caramel ice cream.
I *saw* my cousins playing with a colourful beach ball in the ocean.
I *heard noisy* children screaming that their sandcastle got knocked down.
I *smelled* delicious hot dogs made from the fast food van.
I *felt* the smooth surface of an empty clamshell with salt water inside.
I *tasted* seaweed sushi but it was salty, sour and stretchy.

Next time, beautiful beach, I hope to see noisy seagulls, *hear* scuttling crabs, *smell* vinegar scented chips, *feel* the blue, shiny sea and *taste* crispy, golden cod.

Tahnée Heagarty-Grant (7)

Halloween Disco

I can see a vampire statue that has a red cape, red eyes and a black dress.
I can hear a colourful, dramatic disco that has lots of people.
I can smell strong, dark and grey smoke that covers the whole room and I can smell crackling candles.
I can feel an orange, bumpy pumpkin that is placed on the table.
I can taste sugary sweets I bought with my money at the disco.

Megan Pham (6)
Kingsley Primary School, Northampton

It's Dinner Time

I can see the water boil, bubble, pop and simmer.
I can hear my mum as she prepares our tummy filler.
I can smell my favourite tea as it begins to simmer.
I can feel my tummy rumble, gurgle and jitter.
I can taste all the flavours of my favourite dinner.

Eden Krupnik (6)
Kingsley Primary School, Northampton

Winter

I can see snow falling on the ground.
I can hear lovely Christmas songs.
I can smell yummy cookies in the oven.
I can feel my cold hands after playing with snow.
I can taste a delicious Christmas dinner.

Andreea Mirea (7)
Kingsley Primary School, Northampton

Airport

I can see a humongous, magnificent plane that is waiting to land.
I can hear noisy, loud people who are angry because they missed their flight.
I can smell delicious, beautiful food that is magnificent.
I can feel a comfortable seat that is waiting for me.
I can taste delicious food being served on the plane.

Zayaan Ahmed (7)
Marlborough Infant School, Small Heath

Seaside

I can see clear, wriggling jellyfish swimming in the ocean.
I can hear the loud, blue, roaring ocean waves screaming loudly.
I can smell spicy chicken, it's making my mouth water.
I can feel golden, grainy sand shining brightly.
I can taste cold, delicious ice lolly dripping down my chin.

Taibah Sarfraz (7)
Marlborough Infant School, Small Heath

Beach

I can see children playing with the soft sand.
I can hear loud, noisy seagulls flapping their wings in the sky.
I can smell fresh, beautiful fish and chips.
I can feel the warm sand going through my fingers.
I can taste the freezing, cold ice cream on my tongue.

Muhammad Raiyan Zaman (6)
Marlborough Infant School, Small Heath

Airport

I can see a humongous, cool aeroplane.
I can hear loud, roaring engines all around.
I can smell lots of dusty, black smoke coming from the aeroplane.
I can feel comfy, nice chairs that people can sit on.
I can taste scrumptious, yummy snacks that are expensive.

Ibraheem Ramzan (6)
Marlborough Infant School, Small Heath

Airport

I can see huge, white aeroplanes passing by.
I can hear loud, roaring engines ready to fly.
I can smell smoky, dusty air all around.
I can feel the small, dirty chairs when I sit down.
I can taste delicious, yummy snacks when I get on the plane.

Mohamed-Amin Salad (7)
Marlborough Infant School, Small Heath

Beach

I can see kids playing in the soft sand.
I can hear hungry seagulls flying in the air looking for food.
I can smell tasty fish and chips being freshly made.
I can feel the sea dripping on my body.
I can taste the tasty ice cream melting in my mouth.

Ruqaya Mohamed (7)
Marlborough Infant School, Small Heath

Airport

I can see groups of people rushing towards the huge plane.
I can hear the loud aeroplanes getting ready to take off.
I can smell delicious pizza and ice cream being made.
I can feel the hard chairs when waiting for the plane.
I can taste the cold drink.

Binyamin Toseef (7)
Marlborough Infant School, Small Heath

Beach

I can see a boy surfing on the huge waves.
I can hear seagulls flying in the clear sky.
I can smell fresh, green seaweed when I am near the water.
I can feel soft sand in my hand when I build a sandcastle.
I can taste some delicious food being made.

Salihah Mahmood (6)
Marlborough Infant School, Small Heath

Beach

I can see lots of children having so much fun at the sunny beach.
I can hear children splashing in the water.
I can smell some tasty fish and chips.
I can feel the nice, bright sun on my hand.
I can taste some cold ice cream melting in my mouth.

Hanifah Husayn (6)
Marlborough Infant School, Small Heath

Airport

I can see the small aeroplane in the sky.
I can hear people listening to their loud videos while waiting for their flights.
I can smell yummy food on the plane.
I can feel my passport in my hand.
I can taste tasty, smooth bananas in my mouth.

Saleha Zaman (6)
Marlborough Infant School, Small Heath

Airport

I can see huge, white aeroplanes flying in the sky.
I can hear loud, roaring engines starting to take off.
I can smell dusty air filling the sky.
I can feel clean seats ready for sitting on.
I can taste delicious drinks being served.

Rayyan Ismail Ayub (7)
Marlborough Infant School, Small Heath

Zoo

I can see amazing animals passing by.
I can hear birds chirping altogether.
I can smell cheesy chips with chilli sauce.
I can feel furry animals.
I can taste cold ice lolly freezing my tongue.

Ayaan Nawab Khan (6)
Marlborough Infant School, Small Heath

Summer Camp

I can see fun rides rolling by.
I can hear children screaming loudly.
I can smell delicious food.
I can feel my friend's shoulder, playing tag.
I can taste nice, cold Kinder ice cream.

Inaaya Khan (7)
Marlborough Infant School, Small Heath

Funfair

I can see fun rides zooming around.
I can hear people chatting loudly.
I can smell a delicious smoky BBQ.
I can feel my beautiful toy.
I can taste yummy cotton candy tickling my tongue.

Fatima Ayoka Hassan (7)
Marlborough Infant School, Small Heath

Beach

I can see the beautiful, blue sea.
I can hear people talking loudly.
I can smell the burning, warm sand.
I can feel the jagged rocks under my feet.
I can taste spicy and hot food.

Laiba Fatima (7)
Marlborough Infant School, Small Heath

Seaside

I can see the huge, golden sandcastles.
I can hear the bees buzzing.
I can smell the spicy, hot BBQ.
I can feel the hot, golden sand.
I can taste the cold, delicious ice cream.

Haytham Zariet (7)
Marlborough Infant School, Small Heath

Park

I can see the colourful swings.
I can hear birds squeaking up in the tree.
I can smell fresh air around me.
I can feel the soft grass.
I can taste a delicious ice cream.

Mahir N (6)
Marlborough Infant School, Small Heath

Airport

I can see the kind airport staff.
I can hear loud music all around.
I can smell yummy food being made.
I can feel a large suitcase in my hand.
I can taste a cool drink.

Yasin Rahman (6)
Marlborough Infant School, Small Heath

Summer Holiday

I can see the beautiful sunset.
I can hear birds chirping beautifully.
I can smell delicious BBQ.
I can feel soft, beautiful flowers.
I can taste cold, yummy ice cream.

Adiba Syeda Tasnim (7)
Marlborough Infant School, Small Heath

Beach

I can see the blistering sun.
I can hear the crashing waves.
I can smell the fresh water.
I can feel the warm, golden sand.
I can taste the cold, delicious ice cream.

Areesha Shirin (7)
Marlborough Infant School, Small Heath

Pirates

I can see scary pirates.
I can hear angry, loud voices.
I can smell the old, damp chest.
I can feel the smooth skull flag.
I can taste the lumpy, cold porridge.

Asadallah Muset (7)
Marlborough Infant School, Small Heath

Eco-Park

I can see tall, thin, old trees.
I can hear insects buzzing loudly.
I can smell damp, muddy logs.
I can feel wiggly bugs.
I can taste fresh, juicy fruits.

Khadija Islam (7)
Marlborough Infant School, Small Heath

Airport

I can see a big aeroplane.
I can hear a loud engine.
I can smell the yummy food and yummy chips.
I can feel the soft chair.
I can taste cold ice cream.

Moeez Bashir (7)
Marlborough Infant School, Small Heath

Summer

I can see the blue ocean.
I can hear birds chirping sweetly.
I can smell cheesy pizza.
I can feel cold water splashing.
I can taste yummy ice cream.

Rehan Ali Shah (6) & Inaaya Zeb (6)
Marlborough Infant School, Small Heath

Tamworth Castle

I can see the bright, blue sky.
I can hear the blowing wind.
I can smell the fresh air.
I can feel the calm breeze.
I can taste cheesy sandwiches.

Jabbar Hussain (6)
Marlborough Infant School, Small Heath

Summer

I can see the ice cream van.
I can hear the children chatting.
I can smell fresh watermelon.
I can feel the cold air.
I can taste sugary sweet.

Abdullah Haqqanee (6)
Marlborough Infant School, Small Heath

Beach

I can see the big waves.
I can hear the blue ocean.
I can smell salty water.
I can feel the golden, bright sand.
I can taste spicy burgers.

Nishan Singh (7)
Marlborough Infant School, Small Heath

Garden

I can see Mum and Dad.
I can hear the cat crying.
I can smell cheesy Doritos.
I can feel crunchy Doritos
I can taste salted Doritos.

Mohammed Shiras Khan (7)
Marlborough Infant School, Small Heath

Airport

I can see a big aeroplane.
I can hear a loud engine.
I can smell yummy food.
I can feel the soft chair.
I can taste cold ice cream.

Safa Kosar (7), Sofia (7), Denisa (7) & Umair Muhammed (7)
Marlborough Infant School, Small Heath

Holiday

I can see a swimming pool.
I can hear my baby sister crying.
I can smell BBQ.
I can feel sticky chocolate.
I can taste yummy food.

Umar Muhammad (7)
Marlborough Infant School, Small Heath

Shopping

I can see children.
I can hear my baby sister crying.
I can smell chocolate.
I can feel sticky chocolate.
I can taste yummy food.

Abrish Saqib (6)
Marlborough Infant School, Small Heath

Beach

I can see blue water.
I can hear squawking birds.
I can smell cheesy chips.
I can feel warm sand.
I can taste cold ice cream.

Yousaf Khan (7)
Marlborough Infant School, Small Heath

Beach

I can see blue water.
I can hear singing birds.
I can smell cheesy chips.
I can feel warm sand.
I can taste cold ice cream.

Muzamil Wafa (6)
Marlborough Infant School, Small Heath

Sandcastles

I can see sandcastles.
I can hear the sea.
I can smell chips.
I can feel the sand.
I can taste cold ice cream.

Zainab Zahra (7)
Marlborough Infant School, Small Heath

Shopping

I can see people.
I can hear noises.
I can smell fries.
I can feel the cold.
I can taste sweets.

Mustafa Khan (6)
Marlborough Infant School, Small Heath

Forest

I can see big, smooth leaves floating in the salty water.
I can hear bees buzzing across the big, blue sky.
I can smell pink, tiny, little flowers hovering across the wavy water.
I can feel the tiny, little berries rolling into the water.
I can taste blue, tiny berries in the forest

Lilymae Jaggers (6)
Penryn Primary Academy, Penryn

Garden

I can see bright, white clouds moving in the sky.
I can hear bees buzzing in the wind, loudly.
I can smell beautiful, nice flowers dancing in the sun.
I can feel the green, shiny grass standing strong in the soil.
I can taste red, cool apples from my apple tree.

David Seredin (7)
Penryn Primary Academy, Penryn

Football

I can see annoying, green, waving grass rolling on the football.
I can hear my friend shouting while they score a goal.
I can smell the smelly grass in the dirt.
I can feel the wet, splashing football.
I can taste lots of my friends' invisible breath.

Laudus Nesbitt (7)
Penryn Primary Academy, Penryn

Dragon

I can see colourful, bright, bumpy scales on the dragons.
I can hear dragons breathing yellow, bright red fire.
I can smell dragons' stinky breath.
I can feel the spiky, bumpy spikes on the dragon's back.
I can taste the grey smoke.

Ezekiel Demery (7)
Penryn Primary Academy, Penryn

Meadow

I can see bees buzzing, searching for pollen.
I can hear the wind gushing.
I can smell passion fruit, which makes my belly rumble.
I can feel the rough bark, which leaves marks on my fingers.
I can taste pineapple, which is really tasty.

Eva Festorazzi (7)
Penryn Primary Academy, Penryn

Beach

I can see the big blue sea shining on the sand.
I can hear the big waves in the sea.
I can smell the fish and chips cooking in the oven.
I can feel the sea and the sand in the air.
I can taste the hot fish and chips to eat.

Mya Nicholas (7)
Penryn Primary Academy, Penryn

Fantasy

I can see the red, fiery dragon breathing hot fire.
I can hear the big black pack of werewolves howl.
I can smell the big, fat, strong troll.
I can feel the beautiful, fluffy unicorn.
I can taste the shiny, yellow, golden apples.

Zac Dawe (7)
Penryn Primary Academy, Penryn

The Ice Cream At The Beach

I can see the big, blue sea behind me.
I can hear big kids playing with a red and black football.
I can smell strawberry ice cream nearby.
I can feel the sand on my feet.
I can taste vanilla ice cream with hundreds and thousands.

Archie Sargant (6)
Penryn Primary Academy, Penryn

Unicorn Academy

I can see the warm, cosy stables on the academy campus.
I can hear some happy children chatting.
I can smell some lovely orange starbust flowers.
I can feel the beautiful academy walls.
I can taste some yummy skyberry pies.

Helena Blay (7)
Penryn Primary Academy, Penryn

Park

I can see children playing on the equipment.
I can hear birds in the trees crying.
I can smell flowers on the ground growing.
I can feel the wind when I run really fast.
I can taste ice cream when I go to an ice cream van.

Elliot Adams (7)
Penryn Primary Academy, Penryn

Beach

I can see big, brown boats floating on the ocean.
I can hear seagulls chirping on the rocks.
I can smell ice cream in the ice cream truck.
I can feel waves splashing on me.
I can taste fish and chips in the cafe.

Arthur Williams (6)
Penryn Primary Academy, Penryn

The Girl And The Unicorn

I can see lots of fluffy unicorns with the girl.
I can hear running, fluffy unicorns with the girl.
I can smell cotton candy unicorns.
I can feel good, fluffy unicorns.
I can taste cotton candy unicorns.

Meilah Gauld (7)
Penryn Primary Academy, Penryn

Nature

I can see green, brown, beautiful trees.
I can hear blue, pretty birds singing.
I can smell pink, pretty flowers waving in the air.
I can feel green grass waving in the air.
I can taste the calm wind.

Fflur Hoban (7)
Penryn Primary Academy, Penryn

Lexy And The Rabbit

I can see leaves waving in the wind slowly.
I can hear snakes slithering in the grass.
I can smell the fruits in the tree.
I can feel caterpillars crawling on my skin.
I can taste the fruits in the trees.

Loulou Huebner (7)
Penryn Primary Academy, Penryn

The Bird

I can see a bird in a tree with a nest.
I can hear tweeting and the wind.
I can smell lavender and the beautiful birds.
I can feel the grass, bark and leaves.
I can taste the wind and the water.

Leo Nankivell (7)
Penryn Primary Academy, Penryn

Mermaids

I can see the big, hard, shiny, gold shells.
I can hear calm, loud mermaids
I can smell the freezing, cold, soft sea.
I can feel the soft, hot bit of the sand.
I can taste big, red strawberries.

Adelyn Knowles (6)
Penryn Primary Academy, Penryn

Rabbits

I can see a cute little baby rabbit.
I can hear a rabbit eating a crunchy carrot.
I can smell a rabbit in the soil.
I can feel soft, furry rabbits.
I can taste the fruit next to the rabbit.

Scarlett Buringham (7)
Penryn Primary Academy, Penryn

Cats

I can see cute, fluffy cats sleeping on the sofa.
I can hear meowing, purring cats.
I can smell cat food.
I can feel kittens on the bed.
I can taste gammon in the kitchen.

Esmae Vincent (7)
Penryn Primary Academy, Penryn

Park

I can see children playing on the slides.
I can hear children shouting.
I can smell mud, air and food.
I can feel the park equipment and slides.
I can taste water and food.

Ethan Harwood (7)
Penryn Primary Academy, Penryn

Park

I can see children playing in the park.
I can hear shouting in the park.
I can smell mud in the park.
I can feel the swings in the park.
I can taste ice cream in the park.

Mia-Elaine Collick (6)
Penryn Primary Academy, Penryn

Park

I can see the bright blue sky.
I can hear little yellow ducks in a pond.
I can smell beautiful flowers.
I can feel a nice, fluffy blanket.
I can taste yummy food.

Seren Jordon (7)
Penryn Primary Academy, Penryn

Beach

I can see the trees and waves.
I can hear the seagulls.
I can smell the tasty fish and chips.
I can feel the soft sand.
I can taste the delicious fish and chips.

Owen Brown (7)
Penryn Primary Academy, Penryn

Football

I can see black and white footballs.
I can hear people kindly cheering.
I can smell green, bright grass.
I can feel a soft, smooth ball.
I can taste the air.

Alfee Reid (7)
Penryn Primary Academy, Penryn

Rugby

I can see my favourite teammates.
I can hear balls being passed.
I can smell wavy grass on the field.
I can feel my friends.
I can taste the wind on my lips.

Dougie Boughton Rowe (7)
Penryn Primary Academy, Penryn

The Dinosaur

I can see trees waving.
I can hear a roaring T-rex.
I can smell the stinky smell of dinosaurs.
I can feel the scales of dinosaurs.
I can taste tasty meat.

Rory Darroch-Lassey (7)
Penryn Primary Academy, Penryn

Beach

I can see my mum eating.
I can hear the waves crashing.
I can smell vanilla ice cream.
I can feel salty sea water.
I can taste vanilla ice cream.

Lloyd Jackman (7)
Penryn Primary Academy, Penryn

Football

I can see goals and goalkeepers.
I can hear fans shouting.
I can smell the grass and the lines on the grass.
I can feel nerves from the goalkeeper.

Albie Price (6)
Penryn Primary Academy, Penryn

France

I can see the brown Eiffel Tower.
I can hear long, black trains.
I can smell croissants.
I can feel the Eiffel Tower.
I can taste baguette.

Henry Parkinson (7)
Penryn Primary Academy, Penryn

Beach

I can see crabs and fish.
I can hear seagulls and waves.
I can smell the waves and fish.
I can feel crabs and fish.
I can taste the sea.

Frankie Blundell (7)
Penryn Primary Academy, Penryn

Football

I can see grass.
I can hear screams.
I can smell dirt.
I can feel footballs.
I can taste water.

Evie Pattison (7)
Penryn Primary Academy, Penryn

Rat

I can see a big black smile.
I can hear his claws on the wall.
I can smell blood.
I can feel fur.

Grayson Rohleder (6)
Penryn Primary Academy, Penryn

Beach

I can see seaweed.
I can hear birds.
I can smell fish.
I can feel leaves.
I can taste chips

Penny Brenton (6)
Penryn Primary Academy, Penryn

Baking

I can see a hurricane in the bowl.
I can hear my tummy rumbling.
I can smell all the biscuits cooking.
I can feel the warmth in my hands.
I can taste the chocolate chips tickling my tongue.

Alfred Hudson (6)
Radford Semele CofE Primary School, Leamington Spa

Ponies

I can see swishing tails swaying in the gentle breeze.
I can hear trotting hooves clopping along the gravel path.
I can smell the golden hay that spreads dust everywhere!
I can feel the soft fur of the pretty ponies.
I can taste delicious apples that the ponies eat all day long.

Gabriela Traczynska (7)
Shipbourne School, Shipbourne

Summer

I can see some people playing football.
I can hear the sand when I step on it.
I can smell the amazing flowers.
I can feel the tiny bits of sand on my toes.
I can taste delicious ice cream.

Finley Groves (6)
Shipbourne School, Shipbourne

Dogs Are The Best

I can see floppy ears and waggy tails.
I can hear loud barks.
I can smell smelly, muddy paws.
I can feel soft, silky fur.
While I stroke his soft fur, I munch on chocolate biscuits.

Bluebell Martin (6)
Shipbourne School, Shipbourne

Summer

I can see super, super beautiful flowers.
I can hear buzzing bees.
I can smell sun cream.
I can feel the burning hot air.
I can taste super, super yummy ice cream.

Patrick Crowhurst (7)
Shipbourne School, Shipbourne

The Circus

I can see scary and silly clowns.
I can hear shooting cannons.
I can smell salty popcorn.
I can feel gentle elephants.
I can taste wonderful candyfloss.

Esme Martin (6)
Shipbourne School, Shipbourne

Summer

I can see beautiful flowers.
I can hear tweeting birds.
I can smell sun cream.
I can feel the hot, hot, hot sun.
I can taste delicious ice cream.

Christopher Hayton-Vernet (6)
Shipbourne School, Shipbourne

Super Summer

I can see buzzing bumblebees.
I can hear crashing waves.
I can smell sun cream.
I can feel the burning sun.
I can taste delicious ice cream.

Rosie Baker (7)
Shipbourne School, Shipbourne

Cat

I can see a black cat.
I can hear a cat meowing.
I can smell tasty fish.
I can feel soft fur.
I can taste tuna fish.

Isabella Wallace (7)
Shipbourne School, Shipbourne

School Senses

I can see a crazy teacher, she is always smiling.
I can hear children playing outside in the sandpit, filling up their buckets with sand.
I can smell fresh emerald grass, it is shining in the light of the sun.
I can feel the smooth, smelly lavender. When you touch it your hands become really smelly.
I can taste the crisps from snack time and the fresh air.

Jasmine Varney (7)
Stratford-Sub-Castle CE Primary School, Stratford-Sub-Castle

My Lovely School

I can see feathers blowing in the wind,
fluffy, white clouds and rustling trees
I can hear a barking dog, wind whispering,
cars zooming and noisy cars and birds
I can smell the sweet flowers and smooth
leaves, the tasty lunch and the wind blowing
I can feel spiky grass and bumpy bark, and
soft grass
I can taste slippery water and smooth grass.

Lori Legg (6)
Stratford-Sub-Castle CE Primary School, Stratford-Sub-Castle

My Wonderful School

I can see a big, beige bench that is sitting on the little playground under a big tree
I can hear children gossiping very loudly to each other
I can smell the delicious, yummy lunch being cooked by the lovely dinner ladies
I can feel the soft, spiky grass underneath my feet
I can taste the salty crisps in my mouth, they have a crispy texture.

Zoey Lumby (7)
Stratford-Sub-Castle CE Primary School, Stratford-Sub-Castle

Sense Poetry - Wish Upon A Star

My Wonderful School Senses

I can see a smooth, blue bucket in the sand, being filled with sand
I can hear children talking loudly, being very happy and running around
I can smell grass and beautiful flowers, it is a wonderful fragrance
I can feel soft leaves, smooth plants and gritty, rough sand on the playground
I can taste juicy oranges and salty crisps.

Charlie Ormshaw (6)

Stratford-Sub-Castle CE Primary School, Stratford-Sub-Castle

My Five Senses At School

I can see lots and lots of beautiful books inside the big library
I can hear children playing in the sandpit, throwing sand in others' faces
I can smell delicious, juicy chips coming from the kitchen
I can feel the breeze blowing in my face
I can taste a yummy chocolate cookie coming from a packet.

Phoebe Lake (7)
Stratford-Sub-Castle CE Primary School, Stratford-Sub-Castle

All Around Our School

I can see the black circle-patterned matting on the playground
I can hear lovely nice music coming from the classroom
I can smell chips which are great and I love them so much
I can feel spiky fake grass and it is super duper soft
I can taste crunchy Quavers, which are potato and cheese flavoured.

Samuel Murphy (7)
Stratford-Sub-Castle CE Primary School, Stratford-Sub-Castle

School Senses

I can see children chatting and playing happily in the ginormous playground
I can hear the birds singing a lovely tune in the air
I can smell colourful flowers, it's a pretty smell
I can feel the leafy, dark leaves on a spring tree
I can taste the lovely fruit and yummy melted chocolate.

Sophia Badcock (6)
Stratford-Sub-Castle CE Primary School, Stratford-Sub-Castle

My Beautiful School

I can see sparkly shells outside on a water tank
I can hear birds chirping loudly outside in the sky
I can smell leaves twirling quietly on the lovely grass
I can feel sand, it feels soft, smooth and there are shells in it
I can taste fruit lollies, they are very refreshing and icy.

Arthur Elkins (6)
Stratford-Sub-Castle CE Primary School, Stratford-Sub-Castle

My Beautiful School

I can see a lovely teacher walking around the classroom
I can hear the beautiful birds singing outside
I can smell luscious, green emerald leaves
I can feel the spiky, bumpy, lime, soft grass shining in the sun
I can taste the smoky bacon crisps with a meaty smell.

Matilda Crespo (7)
Stratford-Sub-Castle CE Primary School, Stratford-Sub-Castle

Sense Poetry - Wish Upon A Star

My Wonderful School

I can see some books that have lovely writing inside
I can hear beautiful birds chirping so peacefully
I can smell the colourful, fragrant flowers
I can feel the warm breeze that blows around me in the nice weather
I can taste the sweet, juicy apple for my snack.

Cody Hull (7)
Stratford-Sub-Castle CE Primary School, Stratford-Sub-Castle

My Wonderful School

I can see a blue chair and Miss Smith sitting on it
I can hear a buzzy bee buzzing around
I can smell fresh lavender which smells beautiful
I can feel soft sand, and that slips out of my hand
I can taste a Magnum, it's a type of ice cream I like at home.

Lydia Kennedy (6)
Stratford-Sub-Castle CE Primary School, Stratford-Sub-Castle

School Senses

I can see an amazing smiley teacher called Miss Smith
I can hear birds talking to each other
I can smell a white daffodil that smells really sweet
I can feel the soft felt cross on the wall
I can taste my crunchy mini carrots that are a bit sweet.

Ronan Paton (7)
Stratford-Sub-Castle CE Primary School, Stratford-Sub-Castle

My Wonderful School

I can see snowy-white stems growing in the plant
I can hear children enjoying themselves, playing in the sandpit
I can smell the crispy, soft chips made for the children
I can feel the cold birds' nest like ice
I can taste my crunchy snack.

Fern Rusbridge (7)
Stratford-Sub-Castle CE Primary School, Stratford-Sub-Castle

All Around Our School

I can see sparkly grass, like it's flying in the moonlight
I can hear noisy children chatting in the den
I can smell fresh flowers reflecting the light
I can feel a smooth bench
I can taste the little leaves in the tree drifting in the air.

Esther Ewing (7)
Stratford-Sub-Castle CE Primary School, Stratford-Sub-Castle

School Senses

I can see a hard book on the enormous bookshelf
I can hear a lovely bird tweeting as I walk past
I can smell the fresh, crusty chips wafting from the kitchen
I can feel warm and tickly grass on the track
I can taste sweet, jelly dino jems.

Francesca Gibson (5)
Stratford-Sub-Castle CE Primary School, Stratford-Sub-Castle

School Senses

I can see colourful books in the library
I can hear birds' beaks pecking out of their eggs
I can smell red flowers in the garden
I can feel the soft yellow ball that looks like the sun
I can taste chocolate pancakes, yummy and sticky.

Martha Maclean (7)
Stratford-Sub-Castle CE Primary School, Stratford-Sub-Castle

My Wonderful School

I can see a robin flying around, it's red and black
I can hear children shouting in the enormous playground
I can smell lunch and chips, they smell delicious
I can feel the warm sky
I can taste a delicious Chocobreak from snack time.

Nancy Cash (6)
Stratford-Sub-Castle CE Primary School, Stratford-Sub-Castle

Sense Poetry - Wish Upon A Star

My Wonderful School

I can see the tall buildings far, far away
I can hear the children playing outside on the climbing frame
I can smell the fresh air in the high sky
I can feel the smooth, cold handrail
I can taste the juicy apple in the orchard.

Leo Sawyer (7)
Stratford-Sub-Castle CE Primary School, Stratford-Sub-Castle

My Lovely School

I can see the high monkey bars and fluffy, white clouds
I can hear a barking dog and a noisy cat
I can smell the sweet flowers and tasty lunch
I can feel soft, lovely hair and a bristly hairbrush
I can taste metal and grass.

Sophie Hislop (5)
Stratford-Sub-Castle CE Primary School, Stratford-Sub-Castle

My Wonderful School

I can see shiny, colourful boxes
I can hear birds tweeting in the tree tops
I can smell chips that I want to eat so bad, but cannot yet
I can feel soft fabric like feathers
I can taste fruit that is so nice, I love fruit.

Grace Cash (6)
Stratford-Sub-Castle CE Primary School, Stratford-Sub-Castle

At School

I can see the colourful books in the library
I can hear the noisy little children playing around
I can smell the stinky boys' toilets
I can feel the warm breeze blowing around
I can taste the delicious angel cake.

Zara Altin (7)
Stratford-Sub-Castle CE Primary School, Stratford-Sub-Castle

School Senses

I can see Lego shining in the sunlight
I can hear nature everywhere, it is fun
I can smell my snack which smells good
I can feel the air coming into the classroom
I can taste my crisps, chocolate and banana.

Christiano Ayodeji (6)
Stratford-Sub-Castle CE Primary School, Stratford-Sub-Castle

All Around Our School

I can see a big, fluffy, green tree
I can hear children playing and making lots of noise
I can smell nice flowers on the big playground
I can feel the soft, fluffy felt
I can taste my yummy fruity bake.

Aneurin Faulkner (6)
Stratford-Sub-Castle CE Primary School, Stratford-Sub-Castle

My Lovely School

I can see cars and whistling trees
I can hear singing birds and whistling people
I can smell sweet flowers and spiky grass
I can feel spiky hair and fluffy clothes
I can taste sweet hair and Hula Hoops.

Rory Ferguson (6)
Stratford-Sub-Castle CE Primary School, Stratford-Sub-Castle

All Around Our School

I can see colourful books in the library
I can hear birds singing in their nest
I can smell beans and cheese on yummy jacket potatoes
I can feel the breeze on my skin
I can taste a juicy, red apple.

Hollie Blake (7)
Stratford-Sub-Castle CE Primary School, Stratford-Sub-Castle

My Lovely School

I can see a noisy car and the wind
I can hear a barking dog and rustling trees
I can smell the sweet flowers and yummy dinner
I can feel spiky grass and fresh flowers
I can taste the wind and grass.

Rae Goody (5)
Stratford-Sub-Castle CE Primary School, Stratford-Sub-Castle

School Senses

I can see colourful metal fish on the huge blue wall
I can hear noisy birds tweeting in the sunny sky
I can smell fresh, clean clothes
I can feel a smooth heavy rock
I can taste chunky cheese.

Reggie Chant (6)
Stratford-Sub-Castle CE Primary School, Stratford-Sub-Castle

School Senses

I can see my friends
I can hear children talking
I can smell the children's snacks
I can feel the nice, smooth table
I can taste my own food.

Cruz Lampe (6)
Stratford-Sub-Castle CE Primary School, Stratford-Sub-Castle

My Wonderful School

I can see the blue sky
I can hear jungle music
I can smell the chips from my lunch
I can feel soft books
I can taste the melty marshmallows.

Louis Doe (6)
Stratford-Sub-Castle CE Primary School, Stratford-Sub-Castle

School Senses

I can see the beautiful birds
I can hear the lovely wind
I can smell a fruit bar
I can feel the hot grass
I can taste the nice cereal bar.

Arthur Goldring (6)
Stratford-Sub-Castle CE Primary School, Stratford-Sub-Castle

School Senses

I can see colourful books
I can hear playful children
I can smell chocolate cake
I can feel the warm breeze
I can taste a chocolate bar.

Logan Borsos-Grenier (7)
Stratford-Sub-Castle CE Primary School, Stratford-Sub-Castle

At The Nice Beach

I can see the kind people playing in the sand
I can hear big crashing waves in the deep, dark sea
I can smell the yummy sausages
I can feel the nice, smooth sand beneath my feet
I can taste the yummy fish and chips with lots of ketchup on them.

Chloe Harper (6)
The Lantern Community Primary School, Ely

Beach Sand

I can see friendly children playing basketball with an orange ball
I can hear big, noisy waves in the ocean
I can smell salty seaweed growing on the rocks
I can feel the warm sand on the golden beach
I can taste a yummy ice lolly in my mouth.

Emily Curry (6)
The Lantern Community Primary School, Ely

Summer Beach

I can see the yellow, warm sun and bright blue sky
I can hear crashing blue waves and birds tweeting
I can smell sizzling sausages and yummy fish and chips
I can feel flowers waving and cool water
I can taste yummy BBQs and some ice cream.

Elora Vadamootoo (6)
The Lantern Community Primary School, Ely

Beach Fun

I can see the big blue sky above me
I can hear sizzling sausages cooking
I can smell yummy fish and chips, I can't wait to eat them
I can feel hot sand on the yellow floor
I can taste chocolate ice cream in a yellow cone.

Imogen Harris (6)
The Lantern Community Primary School, Ely

Summer

I can see some colourful trees, they are beautiful trees
I can hear sweet songs, they sound like violins
I can smell nice perfume, it smells like lavender
I can feel a soft and fluffy teddy
I can taste a strawberry ice lolly.

Zola Brown (6)
The Lantern Community Primary School, Ely

Summer

I can see buzzing yellow bees on the pink flowers
I can hear blue crashing waves in the wavy sea
I can smell the fresh air floating around
I can feel the hot sun in the sky
I can taste a cold ice pop in my mouth.

Aria McCabe (6)
The Lantern Community Primary School, Ely

Sense Poetry - Wish Upon A Star

Summer Fun

I can see an ice cream van making music
I can hear noisy seagulls flying about
I can smell the fresh air at the beach
I can feel the golden sand on my hands
I can taste chocolate ice cream at the beach.

Caleb Martin (6)
The Lantern Community Primary School, Ely

Summer

I can see the big white clouds in the sky
I can hear the yellow and black buzzy bees flapping in the sky
I can smell the red juicy roses
I can feel the golden sand
I can taste the sweet cotton candy.

Sophie Howlett (6)
The Lantern Community Primary School, Ely

Summer Fun!

I can see a big, blue sky
I can hear noisy seagulls and waving water
I can smell the fresh air
I can feel cold water, salty water and warm sand
I can taste cold ice cream and yummy fish and chips.

Evelyn Young (5)
The Lantern Community Primary School, Ely

Summer In The USA

I can see a freight train running across the tracks
I can hear the cars zooming across Iowa
I can smell the USA
I can feel the growing corn in th golden fields
I can taste the American ice cream.

Max Law (5)
The Lantern Community Primary School, Ely

Summer

I can see the waves crashing against the shore
I can hear the bees buzzing around
I can smell the nectar from the daisies
I can feel the very soft leaves
I can taste my cold chocolate ice cream.

Hector Williams (5)
The Lantern Community Primary School, Ely

Summer

I can see the trees flurrying about
I can hear waves crashing on the rocks
I can smell red, yummy strawberries
I can feel my bestie's hand in my hand
I can taste a yummy ice cold Slushie.

Lorelei Couzins (6)
The Lantern Community Primary School, Ely

Summer

I can see a big sandcastle
I can hear the ice cream van playing music
I can smell salt and seaweed on the rocks
I can feel the hot sand under my feet
I can taste cold ice cream in my mouth.

Linus MacKenzie-Oakes (6)
The Lantern Community Primary School, Ely

Summer

I can see children playing with a beachball
I can hear the ice cream van's music
I can smell green seaweed on the beach
I can feel the hot sand on my feet
I can taste cold ice cream.

George Langford (6)
The Lantern Community Primary School, Ely

Summer

I can see the bright blue sky
I can hear the golden sand whooshing below me
I can smell salty water in the sea
I can feel the soft and fluffy picnic blanket
I can taste cold ice cream.

Frank McCreadie (6)
The Lantern Community Primary School, Ely

Summer

I can see the beautiful, strong nature
I can hear loud crashing wind
I can smell wet, fresh leaves
I can feel cold, golden sandcastles
I can taste an ice-cold refreshing ice cream.

Erin Vivash-Ball (6)
The Lantern Community Primary School, Ely

Summer

I can see unique butterflies
I can hear buzzing, flying, golden bees
I can smell the colourful flowers
I can feel the sand tickling my feet
I can taste lovely strawberry ice cream.

Olive Hatton (5)
The Lantern Community Primary School, Ely

Summer Time

I can see the bright blue sky near the clouds
I can hear yummy, sizzling sausages
I can smell sweet, beautiful flowers
I can feel wet, warm water
I can taste yummy rocket lollies.

Violet Milne (6)
The Lantern Community Primary School, Ely

Summer

I can see green leaves on the trees
I can hear bees buzzing in the breeze
I can smell daisies and yellow pollen
I can feel that soft leaves are green
I can taste white ice cream.

Millie Stammers (5)
The Lantern Community Primary School, Ely

Summer

I can see the bumpy golden sand
I can hear the ice cream van playing music
I can smell sausages cooking
I can feel the lumpy sand under my feet
I can taste the yummy sausages.

Cooper Platt (6)
The Lantern Community Primary School, Ely

Summer

I can see children building sandcastles
I can hear beautiful buzzing bees
I can smell the lovely fresh air
I can feel the hot, yellow sand
I can taste cold ice cream.

Reese Rose (6)
The Lantern Community Primary School, Ely

Summer

I can see the sun burning hot
I can hear the buzzing bees
I can smell the nice, cool ice cream
I can feel the sun burning
I can taste the light, cool ice cream.

Axel Bliss (6)
The Lantern Community Primary School, Ely

Summer

I can see beautiful butterflies
I can hear trees swaying in the breeze
I can smell shops that sell yummy food
I can feel the yellow sand
I can taste Mr Whippy.

Ellinor Johnson (6)
The Lantern Community Primary School, Ely

The Senses

I can see a sandy beach
I can hear the crashing blue waves
I can smell delicious fish and chips
I can feel wet sand in my toes
I can taste cold ice cream.

Charlotte Lloyd (6)
The Lantern Community Primary School, Ely

Summer

I can see flowers whooshing by
I can hear the big crashing waves
I can smell the good-smelling classroom
I can feel cold ice
I can taste sweet ice cream.

Odette Munganyika (6)
The Lantern Community Primary School, Ely

Summer

I can see sizzling sausages on a BBQ
I can hear big, wet waves
I can smell yummy fish and chips
I can feel the warm, hot sun
I can taste yummy ice cream.

Rupert Halls (6)
The Lantern Community Primary School, Ely

Summer

I can see the butterflies flapping
I can hear the waves crashing
I can smell the fresh air
I can feel the soft sand
I can taste the chocolate ice cream.

Beth Harvey (6)
The Lantern Community Primary School, Ely

Summer

I can see the sandcastles
I can hear the bright blue sea
I can smell the sizzling sausages
I can feel the blue sea
I can taste the sweet ice cream.

Harry Skinner (6)
The Lantern Community Primary School, Ely

Summer

I can see the high waves
I can hear the bees buzzing
I can smell the beautiful flowers
I can feel the green leaves
I can taste the cool ice cream.

Ollie Beale (6)
The Lantern Community Primary School, Ely

Summer

I can see white seagulls
I can hear loud, tweeting birds
I can smell yummy fish and chips
I can feel the golden sand
I can taste cold ice cream.

Benjamin Rowlands (6)
The Lantern Community Primary School, Ely

Summer

I can see sandcastles being built
I can hear the water
I can smell chocolate ice cream
I can feel the warm sand
I can taste chocolate ice cream.

Rafe Maudsley-Noble (6)
The Lantern Community Primary School, Ely

Summer

I can see the loud ice cream van
I can hear waves crashing
I can smell the salty sea
I can feel the golden sand
I can taste vanilla ice cream.

Freddie Godsmark (5)
The Lantern Community Primary School, Ely

Summer

I can see a butterfly that is colourful
I can hear bees buzzing
I can smell a BBQ cooking
I can feel the cold sea
I can taste a cold Slushie.

Erin Holmes (6)
The Lantern Community Primary School, Ely

Summer

I can see golden sandcastles
I can hear the green trees rustling
I can smell some flowers
I can feel the trees
I can taste a cold ice cream.

Jake Downton (6)
The Lantern Community Primary School, Ely

Sense Poetry - Wish Upon A Star

Summer

I can see the cool nature
I can hear the warm sea
I can smell roast potatoes
I can feel the golden sand
I can taste my favourite iced tea.

Alex Curtis (5)
The Lantern Community Primary School, Ely

Summer

I can see the bright blue sky
I can hear sizzling sausages
I can smell the salty sea
I can feel the hot sand
I can taste cold ice pops.

Alex Southward (6)
The Lantern Community Primary School, Ely

Summer

I can see the sand and water
I can hear a cat purring
I can smell sunflowers
I can feel the cat's soft fur
I can taste a Slushie.

Logan Jenkins (5)
The Lantern Community Primary School, Ely

Summer

I can see the bright, yellow sun
I can hear tweeting birds
I can smell a BBQ
I can feel the yellow sand
I can taste an ice cream.

Robert Hughes (6)
The Lantern Community Primary School, Ely

Summer

I can see waves splashing
I can hear the wind
I can smell the salty air
I can feel the green grass
I can taste salty chips.

Paul Musson (5)
The Lantern Community Primary School, Ely

Summer

I can see the sunshine
I can hear the ice cream van
I can smell flowers
I can feel smooth waves
I can taste an ice pop.

Eleanor Mullins (6)
The Lantern Community Primary School, Ely

Sense Poetry - Wish Upon A Star

Summer

I can see nature
I can hear the buzzy bees
I can smell sunflowers
I can feel the air blowing on me
I can taste food.

Leo Cattani-Price (6)
The Lantern Community Primary School, Ely

Summer

I can see seagulls
I can hear the ice cream van
I can smell hot dogs
I can feel the sand
I can taste sausages.

Elijah Mekwuye (6)
The Lantern Community Primary School, Ely

Summer

I can see green trees
I can hear the waves
I can smell a BBQ
I can feel the seaweed
I can taste ice cream.

Adam Nash (6)
The Lantern Community Primary School, Ely

Summer

I can see the buzzing bees
I can hear the sea
I can smell flowers
I can feel fluff
I can taste ice cream.

Avighna Verma (6)
The Lantern Community Primary School, Ely

Summer

I can see the sun
I can hear the bees
I can smell my ice cream
I can feel the sand
I can taste ice cream.

Evelyn House (6)
The Lantern Community Primary School, Ely

Summer

I can see trees
I can hear the bees
I can smell the salty sea
I can feel the sand
I can taste cereal.

Aurora Turner (5)
The Lantern Community Primary School, Ely

Summer

I can see the sun
I can hear seagulls
I can smell food
I can feel the trees
I can taste ice cream.

Oliver Gunbie (6)
The Lantern Community Primary School, Ely

Summer

I can see bees
I can hear the wind
I can smell daisies
I can feel leaves
I can taste ice cream.

Seraphina Atkins (5)
The Lantern Community Primary School, Ely

Summer

I can see birds
I can hear birds
I can smell chicken
I can feel the water
I can taste ice.

Daniel Ching (6)
The Lantern Community Primary School, Ely

Summer

I can see water
I can smell food
I can feel the golden sand
I can taste chips.

Jensen Green (5)
The Lantern Community Primary School, Ely

Young Writers Information

We hope you have enjoyed reading this book – and that you will continue to in the coming years.

If you're a young writer who enjoys reading and creative writing, or the parent of an enthusiastic poet or story writer, do visit our website www.youngwriters.co.uk. Here you will find free competitions, workshops and games, as well as recommended reads, a poetry glossary and our blog.

If you would like to order further copies of this book, or any of our other titles, then please give us a call or visit **www.youngwriters.co.uk**.

Young Writers
Remus House
Coltsfoot Drive
Peterborough
PE2 9BF
(01733) 890066
info@youngwriters.co.uk

Join in the conversation!

 YoungWritersUK   YoungWritersCW   youngwriterscw
 youngwriterscw   youngwriterscw-uk

Scan to watch the video!